First published in
the United States in 1990 by
Gloucester Press
387 Park Avenue South
New York NY 10016

Design: David West
Children's Book Design
Editor: Margaret Mulvihill
Picture Research: Cecilia Weston-Baker
Illustrator: Peter Harper

*The author, Catherine Bradley, has contributed to
and edited many books on World War II.*

*The consultant, Dr John Pimlott, teaches War Studies at the Royal
Military Academy, Sandhurst, England. He is the author of many
books on military history.*

Printed in Belgium

Library of Congress Cataloging-in-Publication Data
Bradley, Catherine .
    Hitler / Catherine Bradley.
        p. cm. -- (World War II biographies)
    Includes bibliographical references.
    Summary: Presents the life of the German Chancellor, focusing
on his rise to power, the buildup of the German Wehrmacht, and
his death in 1945 in a Berlin bunker.
        ISBN 0-531-17228-7
        1. Hitler, Adolf, 1889-1945 -- Juvenile literature. 2. Germany --
History -- 1933-1945 -- Juvenile literature. [1. Hitler, Adolf,
1889-1945. 2. Heads of state. 3 Germany -- History -- 1933-1945.
4. World War, 1939-1945.] I. Title II. Series.
DD 247. H5B69   1990
943. 086' 092 -- dc 20
[B]   89-81612 CIP AC

CONTENTS

WORLD WAR II BIOGRAPHIES

HITLER

AND THE THIRD REICH

CATHERINE BRADLEY

Adolf Hitler was the man responsible for engulfing Europe in war in 1939. The war then drew in countries around the globe and became a "total war." Both civilians and the armed forces suffered from the devastation caused by new and horrifying weapons. During the course of World War II some 50 million people died and many millions of others suffered physical and psychological injuries. Although we still live with many of the consequences of that war, many people do not know why and how it was fought. This book looks at Hitler's career and tries to explain how he was able to cause so much destruction.

GLOUCESTER PRESS
New York : London : Toronto : Sydney

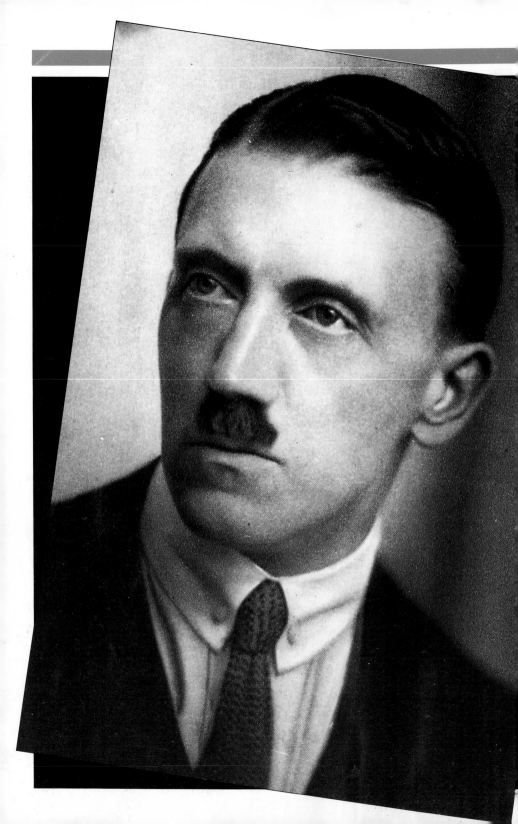

THE FORMATIVE YEARS

Adolf Hitler created a lot of myths around his early life in order to show that he was always destined for greatness. In fact, there was nothing very extraordinary about his background. He was born on April 20, 1889 in the small town of Braunau, which was on the border between Austria and Bavaria. At that time Austria was the most important component of the vast Habsburg Austro-Hungarian Empire, which contained 50 million people and stretched from Switzerland to the Russian empire.

A photograph of Hitler from the 1920s when he was a rising politician. At first he did not like photographs taken of him, but then he appointed a personal photographer to take flattering pictures.

Hitler's father was a customs official and Klara Pölzl was his third wife. Before the marriage she had been the household maid. During Hitler's first five years the family moved several times, finally settling in the neighborhood of Linz in northern Austria. When Hitler was six his father retired. He depicted his father as a bad-tempered drunkard and it is probably true that Alois Hitler, who already had several children from his previous marriages and who was over 50 when Adolf was born, was an unsympathetic father. He died while he was drinking a glass of wine in a tavern. Hitler was not quite 14.

Hitler's difficulties with his father probably arose

Klara Pölzl, Adolf Hitler's mother. He was her fourth child, but the first to survive infancy.

from his poor performance at high school. One of his teachers later remembered "the gaunt, pale-faced youth" as a boy who had "definite talent, though in a narrow field. But he lacked self-discipline, being notoriously cantankerous, willful, arrogant and bad-tempered. He had obvious difficulty in fitting in at school. Moreover he was lazy." But the young Hitler thought of himself as a misunderstood artist, a lonely genius among petty Philistines.

His mother trusted Adolf's idea of himself. On a secure widow's pension she supported her dreamy son when he left school at the age of 16 and tried to become an artist. He continued to live at Linz, drawing, hanging around, reading randomly and listening to the stirring music of Richard Wagner. Hitler adored Wagner's operas with their capacity to arouse great nationalist sentiments and he identified with this composer as another neglected genius whose belief in himself eventually triumphed.

Hitler's class photograph in 1899. He is probably in the middle of the top row. Hitler did well at primary school, but at high school he did not impress his teachers.

In 1907 Hitler left Linz for Vienna, the magnificent capital of the empire. He hoped to be accepted as a student painter at the Academy of Fine Arts. But he did not have enough talent to be admitted, and without a school leaving certificate he could not apply to study architecture, his other favorite subject. Three months after his arrival in Vienna his mother suddenly died. Hitler was disconsolate. He probably had not told her about his rejection by the Academy. The family doctor reported that he had never seen a young man "so crushed by anguish and filled with grief."

Now began the most miserable and lonely five years (1908-13) of Hitler's life. Although he had an inheritance and an orphan's pension, he could not break into the kind of society he thought himself destined for. Instead of joining the artists and the writers and the philosophers in the great cafes of the city center, Hitler, if he mixed with anyone, was in the seediest wine taverns and beerhalls. Not that this particular artist indulged in any of the vices traditionally associated with Bohemianism. Hitler did not smoke or drink, and he did not have girlfriends. He continued to read voraciously in libraries and to have delusions about his genius. He even had a go at writing a Wagnerian-style opera. Still he hoped to get in to the Academy, but again he was rejected.

At the end of 1909, Hitler's family money ran out. Now he was left with nothing to sustain his fantasies. He lived in the cheapest shelters and his few acquaintances were equally down and out. Even among them he was regarded as a hot-tempered eccentric. He eked a small living from selling his postcard paintings of Vienna scenes and from odd jobs, but he was never far from hunger and cold. These lonely, desperate years in Vienna were crucial for the development of Hitler's political ideas. Most important, it was as a social reject in that capital that he developed his hatred of the Jews.

In Vienna's high society there were the aristocratic Jewish families, prominent in the empire's economic life, among the professional classes and as patrons of the arts. At the bottom, in crowded slums, there were the newer Jewish immigrants from eastern parts of the empire. Like Hitler, these poor Jews were trying to make it in the big city. Indeed it was a cliché in Vienna that the children of humble peddlers became industrialists and bankers, that their children became professionals, lawyers and doctors, and that their children became artists and intellectuals. Small wonder that Hitler, the half-educated provincial with a passionate belief in all things purely German, should resent the cosmopolitan Jews of Vienna.

There was nothing unusual about anti-Semitism in Vienna. The city had a famous anti-Semitic mayor, Karl Lueger. But Hitler was an unusually fanatical anti-Semite. By comparison, Karl Lueger's anti-Semitism was very opportunist. It was politically convenient to use the Jews as scapegoats for economic and social ills, but Lueger once declared: "I decide who is a Jew and who isn't." Hitler was obsessed with the Jews. He saw a Jewish conspiracy all around him. The Jews dominated the world of art which had rejected him, and the world of socialism, so unGerman with its emphasis on international links between workers, and inspired by a Jewish theorist, Karl Marx. It did not matter that the family doctor in Linz, who kindly bought some of his pictures, was Jewish. As he hung around Vienna in filthy old clothes, cold and hungry and angry, Hitler thought he knew why greatness had not yet been thrust upon him.

World War I and after

In 1913 Hitler moved to Munich, the capital of the German state of Bavaria. He probably went there to avoid conscription into the Austrian army, but the police did catch up with him and he was returned to Austria for examination. However, he was found to be physically unfit for military service so he went back to Munich.

Later in August 1914, World War I broke out. Now Austria and Germany were at war with Russia, Britain and France, and Hitler was overjoyed. The war was the answer to his aimlessness: "I fell down on my knees and thanked heaven with all my heart." He now had a purpose, to defend Germany (his adopted country). After ten weeks of training he became an army runner, taking messages from the front line to the regimental headquarters. This job required courage and he won two Iron Crosses for bravery. His military role suited his personality. Running to and from the battle meant that he did not have to join in regimental life. The other soldiers called him the "Pipe Dreamer" and remembered him as a loner who was uninterested in alcohol or women.

When the German armistice was announced, in November 1918, Hitler was in a military hospital recovering from temporary blindness after a British gas attack. He was devastated by the news. For him, as for many other German soldiers, the people, who were still willing to fight on, had been let down by lily-livered politicians. After he had recovered from his wounds he spent a month as a guard at a prisoner-of-war camp. Then it was back to chaotic and demoralized Munich, which was full of other malcontents.

After the war Germany was in turmoil. There were several unsuccessful attempts at a Bolshevik-

Hitler with his regimental companions during World War I. He was made a corporal but did not get promotion because his superiors felt he had no leadership qualities.

style revolution in Berlin and elsewhere, while bands of right wing ex-soldiers, known as *Freikorps* (Free Corps), kept the "peace" by murdering their political opponents in broad daylight. The government of the new Republic, called the Weimar Republic after the place where its constitution had been drawn up, had little control over events in the streets. Its first action was to sign the Treaty of Versailles in 1919, which outlined the conditions for peace. Germany lost 13 percent of its territory, including Alsace and Lorraine, and all of its overseas possessions. It could no longer have more than 100,000 soldiers in its army and it would have to pay damages, or reparations, to the victors. These terms, and the government which accepted them, were very unpopular. Also after World War I the League of Nations was set up to prevent war and encourage international cooperation.

Munich was particularly associated with nationalist rather than communist opposition to the Weimar government. In March 1920 a *coup d'état* by the army established a right wing regional government for Bavaria. It was in an atmosphere of plots and violence, and virtual civil war between right and left, that Hitler went to a meeting of the German Workers' Party. He went there in his capacity as an army "instruction officer" who had to keep a watch out for subversive socialist or anti-nationalist ideas among soldiers. Within days he had become a card-carrying member. By the beginning of 1920 he was in charge of the small party's propaganda.

According to Hitler, he had at last found his vocation: "My own fate became known to me...I decided to go into politics." He put his artistic leanings to good use, taking great care over the party's visual image. To irritate the left, red was chosen as the party's color and Hitler borrowed the distinctive swastika emblem from an Austrian group. Moreover, the German Workers' Party now had a new name. It became the National Socialist German Workers' Party, Nazi for short.

In fact Hitler did not like the idea of a political "party," which smacked of socialism. He preferred to think of his Nazis as a movement. He did not remain a background organizer for long. He soon discovered himself as a powerful public speaker. Bigger and bigger halls had to be hired so that an increasing number of people could hear Adolf Hitler expounding a political program which neatly combined anti-Semitism with anti-Marxism. Hitler was never a great theorist, but he instinctively knew how simple ideas, repeated over and over again, worked best on a mass audience. He also knew how to appeal to the emotions of his listeners, how to reassure them that they were not to blame for Germany's ills. It was all the fault of the Jews, the communists and socialists. The natural unit of mankind was the *Volk* (race), of which the Germans were the greatest representatives. Democracy, socialism, liberalism, these forces weakened the master race, which needed strong leadership in order to be great again.

A disaffected army captain, Ernst Röhm, was now sending Hitler arms, followers and funds. Money was raised for a weekly newspaper and Hitler was acknowledged as *unser Führer* (our leader) in July 1921. At his rallies the party's military members, with their distinctive uniforms and salute, were threateningly present. At first these military members were known as the sport division, but soon they were known as the SA (*Sturm Abteilung*, or stormtroopers). Hitler used this private army to terrorize the left in Munich and to extend the party's influence throughout Bavaria.

All of the Nazi leader's appearances were carefully stage-managed. Posters would announce the great event. Then there would be banners, marching music, lots of singing until finally, when the crowd was mad with expectation, Hitler himself would appear. From 1922 he began to hold eight, ten or even 12 political rallies on a single evening. Hitler, once the eccentric outsider, was now a central figure in Munich's political life. Many of the people who supported him were very respectable.

The "Beer Hall" Putsch of 1923

In November 1923 Hitler tried to overthrow the state government of Bavaria. After this local takeover, he hoped to march with his movement on Berlin and establish a Nazi regime throughout Germany. But even though he had powerful backers, this *Putsch*, or coup, failed. It disintegrated when the Bavarian police opened fire on a Nazi demonstration, killing 16 of Hitler's supporters who were destined to become martyrs of the Nazi movement. Hitler escaped by running away, but within days he had been arrested.

At his trial Hitler, whose part in the *Putsch* had been distinctly unheroic, still managed to present himself as a patriotic hero. Although he was sentenced to five years in jail, he only served nine

Publicity promoting Hitler's book *Mein Kampf*. The book was badly written and very muddled, but it did state Hitler's intention to purge Germany of the Jews, who were blamed for the fatherland's misfortunes. It also stated Hitler's intention to tear up the Treaty of Versailles and find *Lebensraum* (living space) in the east for the German-speaking people of eastern Europe.

months. In the Landsberg prison, outside Munich, he was allowed to have as many visitors as he wanted and he used the time to write up his memoirs. Rudolf Hess, a fellow prisoner, worked as his secretary. On Hitler's release this work was published as *Mein Kampf* (My Struggle).

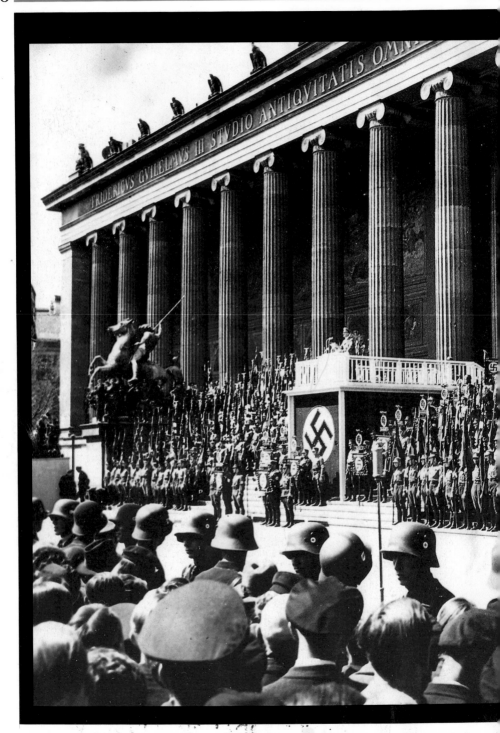

THE THIRD REICH

Within nine years Hitler had become Germany's chancellor and dictator. How did an obscure local politician achieve such an astonishing rise to power? Why were the Nazis allowed to become so all-powerful? It was because most Germans were not sorry to see the end of the uninspiring Weimar Republic, of years of confusion and constant elections. Hitler seemed a decisive and dynamic leader, and if he got out of hand, senior nationalist politicians were still sure that they could control him. Besides, despite the intimidation and terror practiced by the Nazis, they won the November 1932 election. The only body strong enough to resist them was the army, and the army was reluctant to move against a legal government that was in its favor.

Hitler lost no opportunity to stage spectacular ceremonies. Every year the Nazi Party held a rally at Nuremberg. Hitler thought these shows of strength would impress the masses and win them over.

Hitler had been determined that the Nazi movement would come to power legally. But as the Weimar Republic stabilized in the middle and late 1920s, the Nazi vote declined. The Depression of 1929 was good news for Hitler and he got financial support from leading industrialists. In alliance with another far right nationalist, Alfred Hugenberg, who had huge resources at his disposal, including a whole network of newspapers and news agencies, the Nazis became powerful throughout Germany. By 1932 the Nazis were the largest party with nearly 14 million votes. As their leader, Hitler became chancellor of a coalition government of the whole of Germany in January 1933. Then, in a matter of weeks, the *Reichstag*, the German parliamentary building, was burned down. A Dutch communist, Marinus van der Lübbe, was accused of setting fire to the *Reichstag*. The fire gave Hitler an excuse to introduce emergency laws to strengthen his position. By the Enabling Act of March 23, 1933 he became the dictator of Germany.

Hitler now set about creating the Nazi state, the Third Reich. Within four months, all other political parties were banned or had been disbanded. Leading politicians were arrested and detained in concentration camps. By a process known as coordination, or *Gleichschaltung*, many other public institutions were brought under direct Nazi control. Workers had to join a new German Labor Front instead of their trade unions. Ex-soldiers' organizations were merged with the SA. As Minister of Propaganda, Joseph Goebbels controlled radio, newspapers and magazines, so that they all offered the Nazi version of current affairs.

gegen die jüdische
Greuelpropaganda,
kauft
nur bei Deutsch...

Germans defe...
yourselves against je...
atrocity propagan...
buy only at German...

The new Ministry of the Interior made all German universities and schools teach the same virulently nationalist syllabus. All teachers had to join the National Socialist Teachers' Organization. Employers had to join the Estate of German Industry and all German industries became part of the Reich's Economic Chamber.

The Nazis were synonymous with rabid anti-Semitism. Before 1933 they boycotted Jewish shops, attacked synagogues and assaulted individuals. Now the government authorized a systematic persecution of Jewish Germans. But before introducing anti-Jewish laws, which encouraged Jewish emigration by denying civil liberties, Hitler made sure that the Christian churches would not make any effective protest. In July 1933 he signed a Concordat with the Roman

Anti-Jewish posters on a shopfront. In 1933 when the Nazis first came to power, they organized a boycott of Jewish shops. However, it was abandoned soon after because it undermined the economy – something Hitler was reluctant to do. In 1935 the anti-Jewish Nuremberg Laws were passed which denied Jews their rights.

Hitler with Joseph Goebbels (center) and Hermann Göring (right). Goebbels was one of the most intellectual Nazi leaders and became minister of propaganda. Göring had aristocratic connections and had been a World War I fighter pilot and hero. He gave the Nazi leadership upper class appeal.

Catholic Church, which freed that church of state interference in its affairs. However, many of the Catholic clergy did continue to challenge Nazi ideas. Hitler encouraged the Lutheran churches to join his *Reichskirche* (State Church), but one group resisted and formed the Confessional Church, which continued to oppose Hitler.

Hitler still saw himself as an artist and he took a great personal interest in cultural matters. Soon after he took power, books by anti-Nazi writers were burned and some 6,500 paintings were removed from public museums and galleries. Writers and artists were supervised by the Reich Chamber of Culture, which was set up by

Goebbels. Intellectuals now joined the Jews and socialists who had emigrated. To control leisure and youth, the Hitler Youth was set up, with the half-American Baldur von Schirach as its leader. It was run along military lines, effectively training boys to be Nazi soldiers. By 1938 the Hitler Youth had about seven million members and the remaining four million youths were ordered to join.

To stay in power Hitler had to be careful not to provoke a general uprising against his regime. For example, he could not risk reducing wages or raising prices. For his first few years in power he was cautious when it came to the economy and foreign policy. Also, Hitler, who had been a lazy schoolboy and an aimless drifter, now tried to keep regular working hours. But it didn't last. After a while he went back to his old "artistic" routine of sleeping late and working in fits.

Hitler liked to escape for weekends to his house in the Bavarian Alps. Ever since the Nazis had become a national movement his personal life had become more comfortable. He installed his widowed half-sister, Angela Raubal, as his housekeeper. Hitler fell in love with her daughter, Geli, but in 1931 his possessiveness had driven this young woman to suicide. For weeks after Geli's death Hitler was inconsolable, and his vegetarian-ism dated from that trauma. Later, Eva Braun became his mistress. A former shop assistant, Eva Braun was a sporty, outdoor girl, but Hitler did not allow her any public role. Eva was kept firmly in the background. Her main appeal was her dogged loyalty to him and he only married her on the day before their joint suicide in 1945.

Contrary to the image of a round-the-clock *Führer* with eyes at the back of his head, Hitler did not keep tabs on everything and everyone. He was happy to delegate, leaving the day-to-day running of Germany to his chosen ministers and personal staff. Hermann Göring was prime minister of Prussia, commander-in-chief of the air force and head of a four-year plan to improve the German economy. Heinrich Himmler was head of the police and chief of the Nazi elite guard, the *Schutzstaffeln*. Joseph Goebbels was minister of propaganda and chief of Berlin. Rudolf Hess was Hitler's deputy, a minister and ran the *Führer's* personal staff. Each of these men had regular access to Hitler and they carried out his orders, but often they were left to run things on their own and sometimes plotted against each other for more power. This was a trait of the Nazi administration. Because Hitler could not be bothered to supervise matters properly, there was little coordination and much overlapping of duties. Although outside observers often thought that the Nazi state was efficiently run, this was in fact not the case.

The Night of the Long Knives

Rivalries between the army and the SA led to the Nazi state's first crisis in 1934. Ernst Röhm, the leader of the SA, was disappointed that Hitler had not started a more thorough-going Nazi revolution. He wished to see the SA, the military body which had facilitated the rise of the Nazis, incorporated into the German Army.

But the *Führer* had other ideas, and Röhm was an embarrassing reminder of the past. Hitler wished to rearm and rebuild the German Army, to introduce conscription, for example, so that all of Germany's young men would have a military training. Now that he had power as the elected ruler of Germany he could begin to infiltrate and work with the existing army. There was no need to turn the SA into the basis of a new, rival "people's army." But that was what Röhm was pushing for, and now Hitler had to be rid of him. With the backing of Göring, Himmler and Hess, Hitler planned to eliminate the SA and its leader. On June 30, 1934 he arranged to meet with Röhm. But instead of a meeting there was a bloodbath. Röhm and about 150 SA leaders were executed by the SS during the night. At the same time SS execution squads settled other scores, moving in against Hitler's old enemies. This action took place on June 29/30. It became known as the "Night of the Long Knives" and it is thought that a thousand people died.

The army leaders, pleased to see the elimination of the SA which had rivaled them, supported this action. When President Paul von Hindenburg died, in August 1934, they agreed to a merging of the office of chancellor with the office of president. That meant that Hitler was the supreme head of the armed forces of the Reich. German soldiers now took their oath of loyalty to the *Führer*.

Although Hitler's long-term aims were clear, to achieve them he did not have a clear-cut, detailed program. However, it was obvious that a Germany fit to wage war had to be a strong Germany, and the economy was organized to this end. Public works, such as the building of the new road network, the *Autobahnen*, provided good publicity for his regime, and in the future they would also have their military uses. More of the German economy was geared up for war than was the case in any other European country. However, by 1938 living standards in Germany were falling because of spending on arms. By the time World War II began, Germany was facing an economic crisis. War made some immediate economic sense because Germany could then seize food and raw materials, such as oil and metals, from overseas.

The Third Reich and the world
Whereas Hitler left the running of internal matters to his ministers, when it came to foreign affairs he took a leading part. In spite of his well-known long-term aims – rejection of the Versailles Treaty, *Lebensraum* and German rearmament – Hitler proceeded cautiously at first. He followed the policies of his predecessors in office, waiting for the right moment. Just as he knew how to manipulate the emotions of mass audiences, Hitler had a knack for capitalizing on the weaknesses of other states. It was 1935 before he openly announced that he could no longer respect the Treaty of Versailles and that he was going to rearm Germany. By then he knew that because of their own internal difficulties and because they were more frightened of Soviet Russia than fascist Germany, France and Britain, for all their protests, would not stop him. Hitler used all his talents as a propagandist to persuade them that he was a man of peace, an ally against the rise of communism who was only concerned to remove the acknowledged injustices of the Versailles Treaty. By signing a naval pact whereby Germany was

allowed to have a navy up to 35 percent of the strength of the British one, Britain agreed to German rearmament.

Italy also had a fascist dictator in the shape of Benito Mussolini. Ever since he had come to power, in 1922, Mussolini had been seeking to increase Italy's power and prestige. When Italy invaded Ethiopia in 1935 Hitler watched with interest. He saw that in spite of protests from the League of Nations, the other powers did nothing to stop this invasion. Although he stayed neutral, immediately after the invasion he began to negotiate for an alliance with Italy. The Anti-Comintern Pact between Germany and Japan was formed in November 1936, and in the following year Italy joined. Hitler was now secure enough to send German troops in to reoccupy the Rhineland, from which they had been excluded by the Treaty of Versailles. This act was done in defiance of Britain and France, but the governments of these countries were not prepared to risk a war.

Hitler with Benito Mussolini, the fascist dictator of Italy. He proved a natural ally for Hitler, and joined him in the Anti-Comintern Pact in 1937. In May 1939 Mussolini and Hitler signed a formal alliance, known as the Pact of Steel.

The outbreak of civil war in Spain in 1936 provided Germany and Italy with military and political opportunities. In aiding General Francisco Franco's forces, Hitler had a chance to test some of Germany's new armaments. Spain became a training ground for the *Luftwaffe* (Germany's air force). Meanwhile the Soviet Union helped the beleaguered Republican forces, who got no assistance from Britain and France.

In January 1938 Hitler took control of his armed forces by getting rid of two senior generals and making himself commander-in-chief of the army. Hitler then sent his army into Austria, and annexed it in the *Anschluss* (Union). Chancellor Engelbert Dollfuss of Austria had been murdered in 1934 on Hitler's orders and since 1936, the Nazis had dominated the country of the *Führer's* birth.

After the success of the *Anschluss* Hitler planned the acquisition of *Lebensraum* in the east. The Austrian-born *Führer* was full of contempt for Czechoslovakia, an independent nation created in the aftermath of World War I. The Czechs and the Slovaks, like the Poles, were Slavs, inferior in every way, so Hitler believed, to the German master race. Now he wished to annex the German-speaking Sudetenland area of Czechoslovakia, and he threatened war if the other powers did not allow this. The British prime minister, Neville Chamberlain, acted as an intermediary between Germany and an outraged Czechoslovakia. In September 1938 Chamberlain, Hitler, Mussolini and the French prime minister, Edouard Daladier, met at Munich to resolve the crisis, but the Czechoslovakian government was not represented.

The result was an agreement by which Hitler was allowed to break up Czechoslovakia in return for promising not to occupy the non-German-speaking regions of that country. The Munich Agreement was hailed as a triumph for diplomacy and peaceful negotiation. Neville Chamberlain spoke of "peace with honor." But soon it was clear that there had been no triumph. In March 1939 the German Army marched into the rest of Czechoslovakia and seized the city of Memel from Lithuania. It was obvious that there was no point in appeasing Hitler. Now Poland, in Hitler's opinion a "ridiculous state" which also contained some ethnic Germans within its borders, was within his sights.

To many western politicians, communism, rather than fascism, was the real threat to the world order. When the Soviet Union emerged from a period of isolation in the mid-1930s, its leader, Josef Stalin, was concerned to make an alliance with other states against Nazi Germany. But this did not happen since Britain and France were wary of the Soviet Union. In August 1939 the world was stunned by news of the non-aggression pact signed by Hitler and Stalin. In effect, this meant that there would be no Soviet resistance to Hitler's invasion of Poland, if the Soviet Union itself benefited from the resulting carve-up. On August 31, the German Army staged an incident on the border with Poland. The next day there followed a spectacular *Blitzkrieg* (lightning war) and it looked as if Poland would go the way of Czechoslovakia. But Britain and France were committed to defending Poland. After years of appeasement, they had no choice but to declare war on Germany. World War II had begun.

BLITZKRIEG

Blitzkrieg is the German word for lightning war and it is used to describe the highly mobile method of warfare adopted by the German Army in the early years of World War II.

In the 1930s a group of British military thinkers, including Captain Basil Liddell Hart, worked on ideas of tank warfare. The German Army used the same tactics of cutting off the enemy from supplies and communications. In the first phase aircraft were used to soften up and terrorize the enemy. Then tanks were rushed in to envelop the enemy and force it to surrender. Surprise and fear were major elements of *Blitzkrieg*.

In 1939 the tactic was used with great success in the Polish campaign. The land was very flat and ideally suited to tank warfare. General

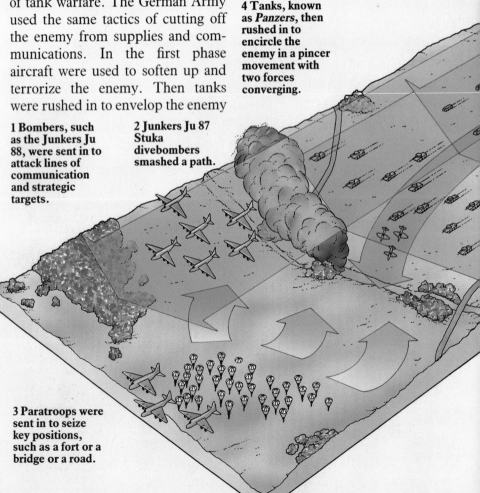

4 Tanks, known as *Panzers*, then rushed in to encircle the enemy in a pincer movement with two forces converging.

1 Bombers, such as the Junkers Ju 88, were sent in to attack lines of communication and strategic targets.

2 Junkers Ju 87 Stuka divebombers smashed a path.

3 Paratroops were sent in to seize key positions, such as a fort or a bridge or a road.

Heinz Guderian was Hitler's armored warfare expert and he suggested high-speed warfare in the Soviet Union in 1941. The tanks would have been sent hundreds of miles in advance of the infantry. The leading members of the German High Command thought this too risky and did not try it.

5 Motorized infantry then followed up the tanks and took prisoners or seized equipment.

The Junkers Ju 87 Stuka divebomber could go into a steep dive and release its bombs accurately on its target. It had sirens fitted so when it was diving it terrified the people below.

A *Panzer* III advances through Soviet territory in 1942. As long as the Germans had superiority in the air, the tanks could advance rapidly and cut the enemy off from its base.

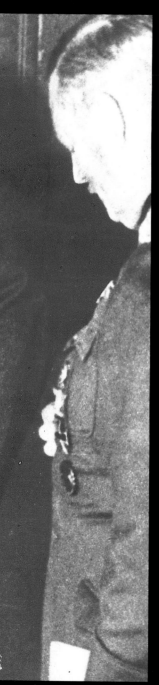

THE WARLORD

For the first two years of the war Germany, and Hitler in particular, looked like the winner. Although the Poles had more than a million soldiers, they were generally hampered by lack of transportation. The German air force easily destroyed the obsolete Polish aircraft on the ground, as well as bombing the railway system.

Hitler with his generals. On the left is General Friedrich Paulus who earned Hitler's anger when he surrendered to the Soviets in February 1943. Hitler's relations with his generals were stormy.

By September 17 the Polish capital, Warsaw, had been encircled and the Soviet Union had invaded from the east. Within a week Poland was overrun and Hitler and Stalin divided the country between them. Although Britain and France had declared war, they had yet to back that declaration with effective action. There followed several months of waiting, known in British newspapers as the *Sitzkrieg*, or "Sitting War." Hitler was eager to push ahead with an invasion of France, but bad weather and opposition from his generals resulted in no less than 29 postponements. To keep his unruly generals in check, Hitler began to hold daily war conferences. At these meetings the *Führer* displayed his detailed interest in every aspect of the war, from lists of ammunition and weapons, to the pros and cons of different strategies. Above all, he was concerned to keep the German war machine mobile. He did not want this conflict to degenerate into the trench warfare he had experienced during World War I. He wanted maximum use of tanks and when other generals had been slow to take this up in 1938, he appointed General Heinz Guderian as commander of the mobile troops.

By the spring of 1940 the German generals had accepted General Erich von Manstein's daring plan for the invasion of France. It involved going through Holland and Belgium to lure the British and French armies north, then sending the main thrust of the German attack through the Ardennes Forest, which the British and the French thought impassable by tanks. But before this invasion, General Nikolaus von Falkenhorst was ordered into Norway. This Norwegian campaign was the first for which Hitler was the supreme commander.

On April 9, 1940 the invasion of Norway began. The Germans had occupied Denmark and used its airbases to attack southern Norway. It started badly with ten German destroyers sunk at Narvik and troops left at the harbor without supplies. Hitler lost his nerve and ordered a withdrawal. However, his chief of staff, General Alfried Jodl, suppressed that order and within a few days German troops had overcome the Norwegian resistance in the south. In mid-April the British sent troops to Narvik and Trondheim, but after a few weeks of fighting they had to withdraw. By the end of June Germany was in control of most of Norway.

The scene was now set for the invasion of France. When the German tanks rolled forward on May 10, the British and French were taken completely by surprise. Although the number of troops on both sides was equal, the Germans had more aircraft, and within six weeks France had fallen. Holland fell in the first five days and then Belgium was overrun. The German advance was so sudden and successful that even Hitler was nervous. He was afraid that the tanks would be cut off if they did not wait for the rest of the army. On May 17, Hitler ordered Guderian's tanks to stop, but the general more or less ignored this order and pressed ahead to Abbeville. Again, on May 24, Hitler lost his nerve and ordered a 48-hour halt. The other army commanders were against this, but Göring, chief of the air force, promised that his aircraft would deal with the Allies and so Hitler had his way. This delay allowed the British to organize the evacuation of troops from Dunkirk in northern France.

Now the German Army turned south, meeting with little opposition and entering Paris on June 14. Within days Marshal Henri Philippe Pétain, who had been a French World War I general, asked for an armistice, and Hitler signed it at Compiègne on June 22. This was where the Germans had surrendered after World War I and to rub in the significance of the French defeat, the same railcar in which the German leaders had been humiliated in 1918 was removed from a museum in Paris so that it could be used for the ceremony.

After this success Hitler was even more sure of himself as a military genius. He exaggerated his military experience during World War I and paid little heed to more expert advice. Because of the success of the western campaign, his generals fell into line behind the *Führer* as his thoughts turned to victory in the east. In his opinion the Soviet Union could be finished off in a four to six-week campaign. But before Germany could focus on that campaign there were a few other problems to deal with.

Against the odds, Britain under its new prime minister, Winston Churchill, was continuing to fight. Moreover, the United States, which was still officially neutral, was aiding Britain's struggle. German U-boats in the Atlantic hoped to starve Britain into submission by harassing the ships bringing such aid, and until 1942 they were very effective in this strategy. But Hitler was mistaken in his underestimation of the power of a possible alliance between his enemies and the United States. In spite of his own alliance with Japan, he tended to think of the war in purely European terms. As a multi-racial, democratic country – "half-Judaized, half-negrified" – the United States would be no match for the master race. But he did not have to worry about the possibility of American forces in Europe for now. Instead, he considered an invasion of Britain. Although Germany did not have enough amphibious craft for this undertaking, Göring was confident that his *Luftwaffe* could wipe out the Royal Air Force (RAF). Accordingly, the all-out offensive against the RAF began on August 13, 1940 (Eagle Day). At first the German attack was concentrated on air bases and radar stations, but on September 7, it switched to London. However, by September 17, the German losses were so high – 71 planes were shot down in one day – that the invasion of Britain had to be postponed.

Still hoping that Britain would eventually see things his way and come to a deal, Hitler concentrated on the east. Already he was master of a large European empire, with massive resources and

A German Messerschmitt fighter plane chases a British Supermarine Spitfire across the skies of Britain. This was a propaganda picture published in the Nazi magazine, *Signal*.

manpower, if not raw materials. During the *Sitzkrieg* Germany had received oil from the Soviet Union and Romania, essential for the campaign against France and Britain. If Germany did not get the Soviet Union's oil, the war industries would grind to a halt and there would be severe economic difficulties. Also, the territories under German control did not produce enough grain – the Soviet Union was a tempting source of food supplies. Despite the Nazi-Soviet pact, Hitler did not trust Stalin, who was moving into parts of eastern Europe and threatening the vital Romanian oilfields. Besides, hostility toward the Soviet Union was essential to the important long-term aim of winning *Lebensraum* in the east and crushing communism. Hitler enjoyed fantasising about the vast new German empire which would replace the Soviet Union.

To prepare for that offensive, Hitler strengthened his alliance with Italy and Japan by signing the Tripartite (Axis) Pact in September 1940. With a US intervention in mind, they each agreed to come to one another's aid in the event of attack by a country not yet officially involved in the war. Italy had entered the war in June 1940, but Hitler found that as an ally Mussolini was a liability. In January 1941 he sent forces under General Erwin Rommel to North Africa to help the Italians there. Although Rommel managed to drive the British back to Egypt, this North African campaign would fester until 1943 as a constant drain on the German military machine. In April and May 1941 German forces overran Yugoslavia and Greece, where the Italians had also been defeated.

The date for Operation Barbarossa, codename for the invasion of the Soviet Union, was set for June 22, 1941. The superstitious *Führer* chose this date because it was the anniversary of the signing of

OPERATION BARBAROSSA

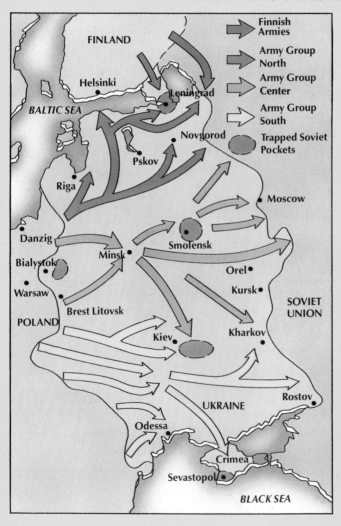

Finnish Armies
Army Group North
Army Group Center
Army Group South
Trapped Soviet Pockets

FINLAND
Helsinki
BALTIC SEA
Leningrad
Novgorod
Pskov
Riga
Moscow
Danzig
Smolensk
Minsk
Bialystok
Orel
Warsaw
Kursk
Brest Litovsk
SOVIET UNION
POLAND
Kiev
Kharkov
Rostov
UKRAINE
Odessa
Crimea
Sevastopol
BLACK SEA

Operation Barbarossa was a three-pronged invasion, which was supposed to be over in a few months. The priority targets were Leningrad in the north, Moscow in the center and the Ukraine and Caucasus in the south. In August Hitler changed his mind and diverted units from Army Group Center to the Ukraine. Before winter he changed his mind again and made Moscow a priority. Moscow held out, but even if Moscow had fallen, it is unlikely that the Soviet resistance would have collapsed. Hitler was so furious when Barbarossa failed that he sacked many generals. The commander-in-chief of the army was sacked and Hitler took his place.

the French armistice. Germany had enough oil for two months of fighting. Hitler was so confident of early victory that no plans were made to equip his soldiers for a Russian winter. The invasion was preceded by an air assault in which half of the aircraft of the Soviet air force was wiped out. There were three invading armies: Army Group North was to push toward Leningrad, Army Group Center to Moscow and Army Group South to the Ukraine and the Caucasus.

This war in the east had an especially vicious, genocidal dimension that was consistent with Hitler's opinion of the Russians as subhumans, like the Jews. Special commando groups, the *Einsatzgruppen*, would go in after the main armies so as to liquidate the "Jewish-Bolshevik ruling class."

German tanks advance into Rostov, 1941. During the summer offensive in 1941, many German soldiers found the heat unbearable.

Immediately, the German armies made rapid inroads into Soviet territory, but there was no easy victory. In the vast expanses of the steppes armored warfare was not as effective as it had been in the west, and the Soviet armies, which the Germans had hoped to encircle, kept slipping away. Also, whereas the German strategists had wagered on 200 divisions of the Red Army, there were 360 divisions. After much disagreement between the *Führer* and his generals about the progress of Operation Barbarossa, German tanks encircled the Soviet armies near Kiev. After heavy fighting, some 500,000 prisoners were taken. But this was not an easy *Blitzkrieg* and worse was to come. As the German tank columns, the *Panzers*, headed for Moscow they got bogged down in mud, snow and inadequate roads. On December 6, 1941 General Georgi Zhukov rallied the Soviet troops to counterattack the Germans in front of Moscow. Without winter equipment the German position became intolerable, but Hitler ordered his troops to stand fast and sacked some of his leading generals.

Meanwhile, Himmler's SS began to prepare for the *Führer's* "New Order" in Europe, by which was meant a Europe without Jews. Already the *Einsatzgruppen* were terrorizing the Soviet Union with great efficiency. The official SS reports, which only detailed a proportion of the atrocities carried out, indicated that nearly 300,000 people had been executed during the first six months of the Russian campaign. The secret police, or *Gestapo*, also run by Himmler, was in charge of screening captured Russian soldiers: of 5,700,000 prisoners, only one million would survive the war.

The smouldering remains of Vitebsk, which is about 315 miles west of Moscow. The Soviets set fire to positions about to fall so that the Germans could not capture anything of use.

There were also constant round-ups of Jews in the other countries under Nazi occupation. They were easily recognizable because of the yellow stars they were forced to display. Along with captured resistance fighters, communists, gypsies, homosexuals, and other "undesirables," Jews were transported to concentration camps. Labor camps for the detention of opponents of the Nazis and other unwanted people had existed since before the war began, but between 1940 and 1942 nine new camps were established. At such prison factories prisoners were worked to death on behalf of the German war effort, but besides these there were also new camps, such as Auschwitz in Poland, which were specially designed for mass murder. Whatever else happened, Hitler was determined on a "Final Solution" to the Jewish "problem."

After Japan's attack on the US Pacific Fleet at Pearl Harbor, in December 1941, Hitler declared war on the United States. But while the Soviet Union, Britain and the United States worked closely together, the Axis powers, Germany, Italy and Japan, did little to coordinate their strategies. Hitler was preoccupied with the east. For the 1942 campaign in Russia he committed his troops to another major offensive. The objective was to capture the vital, oil-rich Caucasus area. By early autumn the German Army was heading for Stalingrad. But the Soviet forces had been able to organize the defense of their second largest city, and instead of a knockout victory there was a protracted battle. In the meantime, Rommel in North Africa was unable to defeat the British, in spite of many successes, and the German Navy did not have enough submarines to stop American and British ships from carrying supplies across the Atlantic. Also, the Allies had begun to bomb Germany itself, damaging war production and demoralizing the civilian population in the cities.

The month of November 1942 proved to be a turning point in the war against Hitler.

THE HOLOCAUST

In the 1930s the Nazis set up labor camps, where people were worked to death. At first, German Jews were sent to these camps or made to leave Germany. When the German Army conquered Poland and western Europe, there were nearly three million Jews in Hitler's power. The Nazi leadership had various schemes for getting rid of the Jews, including sending them to Madagascar. In 1941 the decision was taken to draw up plans for the destruction of the Jews. Experiments in gassing Jews started in 1941 and by 1942 large-scale death camps were built.

Jewish prisoners were sent by train from all over Europe. When they arrived at their destination, they were processed. Their clothes and belongings were removed and their heads were shaved. They were then sent naked into the gas chambers. At first the Nazis buried the bodies, but when it became clear that the Allies would eventually overrun the camps, the bodies were burned so that no trace would be left.

The camps were run by SS officers and guards. They often recruited local people to join the SS and help run the camps. They also used

SCANDINAVIA

Prisoners at Belzec burn boots to keep warm. New arrivals had their boots and clothes taken away. They then went into the gas chambers.

Jewish prisoners to do unpleasant tasks. There were many instances of heroic Jews trying to seize arms and save friends and family. Most Germans did not know about the camps.

Jewish children from Warsaw being transported to a camp. Many people died *en route* as they were not given any food or water for several days.

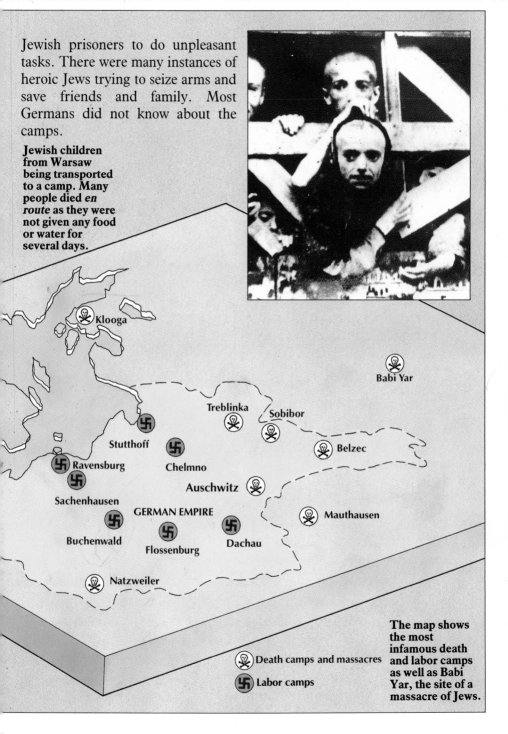

Klooga

Babi Yar

Treblinka

Sobibor

Stutthoff

Belzec

Ravensburg

Chelmno

Auschwitz

Sachenhausen

GERMAN EMPIRE

Mauthausen

Buchenwald

Flossenburg

Dachau

Natzweiler

Death camps and massacres

Labor camps

The map shows the most infamous death and labor camps as well as Babi Yar, the site of a massacre of Jews.

In North Africa Rommel was defeated at El Alamein, while on the Eastern Front the Russians succeeded in encircling the German Sixth Army at Stalingrad. The *Führer* would not allow them to withdraw: "If we abandon it – Stalingrad – we are really abandoning the whole meaning of the campaign." By February 2, 1943, after weeks of frozen siege, Paulus's Sixth Army had surrendered and 91,000 German soldiers were captured.

Hitler's staff were nervous of telling him the bad news. By now he was living in a world of his own. He seldom ventured from his special headquarters, the *Wolfsschanze* ("Wolf's Lair"), at Rastenburg in East Prussia. This depressing complex was set in the middle of a thick and gloomy forest. Hitler's most devoted henchmen could not help noticing how much he had aged in a couple of years. The stress of being a dictator and supreme war leader was beginning to take its toll. To make matters worse, the *Führer* relied on drugs administered to him by a quack doctor, which only aggravated his demented state. After the disaster at Stalingrad, Martin Bormann presented Hitler with an Alsatian dog, Blondi, to cheer him up. Apart from walking this dog, Hitler had no other form of relaxation. Instead of inviting guests for dinner, he ate with his secretaries and they were under strict orders not to mention the war. He refused to visit bombed-out cities, or to read military reports on setbacks. The already strained relations with his generals got worse, while Himmler and the SS grew in power and influence. Although the war would continue for another two and a half years, it was the beginning of the end of the Third Reich.

THE GERMAN EMPIRE

By 1942 Hitler's empire had reached its greatest extent in Europe. The map shows the territory occupied by Hitler as well as Germany's allies and opponents. Although Hitler was the master of enormous resources of materials and labor, he did not have sufficient oil to fuel his war machine. By the end of 1942 Hitler's armies were on the defensive and it was only a matter of time before the Germans were defeated.

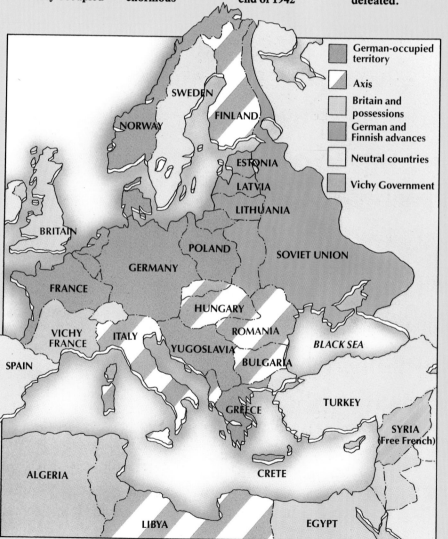

Legend:
- German-occupied territory
- Axis
- Britain and possessions
- German and Finnish advances
- Neutral countries
- Vichy Government

SWEDEN
NORWAY
FINLAND
ESTONIA
LATVIA
LITHUANIA
BRITAIN
POLAND
GERMANY
SOVIET UNION
FRANCE
HUNGARY
VICHY FRANCE
ITALY
ROMANIA
YUGOSLAVIA
BLACK SEA
SPAIN
BULGARIA
GREECE
TURKEY
SYRIA (Free French)
ALGERIA
CRETE
LIBYA
EGYPT

THE FINAL DEFEAT

Hitler accepted the blame for the defeat at Stalingrad, and for the first time in the war agreed to the withdrawal of his armies on the Eastern Front. By the end of February 1943 the strength of the Soviet counterattack had forced the German Army to move 187 miles west. Without adequate numbers of men and tanks, it was on the defensive.

A Soviet soldier unfurls a Soviet flag from the top of the *Reichstag* building in the center of Berlin, April 1945.

V1 AND V2 ROCKETS

Hitler pinned his faith on decisive weapons that would win the war. They were called *Vergeltungswaffen* or vengeance weapons. The V1s were flying bombs which were launched from sites in northern France. The Allies bombed some of the sites and there were production delays so the V1 offensive only started in June 1944. Within a fortnight more than 2,000 had been launched and London and other southern towns were the targets. They were highly inaccurate, but they did kill 6,139 people and were important propaganda weapons.

The V2 rockets had a great range and the first was launched in September 1944 from Belgium to Paris. About 6,000 were produced, of which 1,054 fell on Britain. They were launched from mobile units and killed some 2,855 civilians in Britain.

△ In the photograph above you can see a V1 over the streets of London. They did not produce the civilian panic that Hitler had in mind.

◁ At the end of the war the US Army took a V2 rocket back to the United States for extensive testing. They learned much about rocket technology.

Launch sites

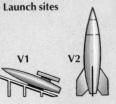

V1   V2

The map shows the principal sites for launching the V1 and V2 rockets at London. The Allies bombed these sites.

After Stalingrad Hitler delivered only two public speeches and he made many decisions which turned out to be wrong. He blocked production of the first jet fighter plane, the Messerschmitt Me 262, which might have stopped the Allied bombers over Germany. Instead, Hitler was convinced that rockets or V-weapons would be the "decisive weapons." Massive resources were put into their development, but in fact they played little part in the war. Defensive weapons, such as ground-to-air missiles, might have slowed up the Allied bombing campaign. At various points, when he knew that the military situation was hopeless, Hitler refused to be realistic, throwing armies into battle against inevitable defeat. In January 1943 the Allies declared that they would not negotiate a peace settlement. Rather, they were seeking Germany's "unconditional surrender" – something Hitler refused even to contemplate.

The tactics of "divide and rule" – having individuals and groups working against each other under his direct control – were not suitable for a defensive war. While Armaments Minister Albert Speer worked hard to organize war production, his efforts were undermined by the SS and by Fritz Sauckel, who was in charge of labor allocation. The rivalry between the Army and the SS continued. From 1942 onward the SS was allowed to build up its own military divisions, known as the Waffen SS, until by the end of the war there were 35 of them. When trains were desperately needed by the Army for troops and equipment, the SS continued to transport Jews to concentration camps. Time was running out for those prisoners who had survived until now. The "Final Solution" would intensify until at least six million Jews had been slaughtered. The death camps were efficiently run, in contrast to the running of the countries occupied by Germany, where there was administrative chaos. For example, Hans Frank was in charge of governing Poland, but Himmler and the Army constantly interfered with his regime.

In the spring of 1943 Hitler was keen, in spite of his generals' forebodings about Germany's lack of resources, to launch a limited summer offensive on the Eastern Front. He wanted to straighten the line at Kursk. But by the time this offensive was launched, on July 5, the Soviet forces were well-prepared: they had built defensive trenches and laid minefields. The German tanks became bogged down and then the Soviet tanks were brought in to counterattack. In the greatest tank battle of World War II, some 3,000 tanks were destroyed and the Germans were firmly pushed back. They also suffered from partisan (local people) attacks on their lines of communication. In August there were 12,000 partisan attacks. The Germans retreated in confusion, leaving utter devastation behind them. On November 6 Kiev was liberated by the Russians, but then the fronts stabilized as the Soviet armies awaited supplies.

During the Kursk offensive a new crisis developed in the Mediterranean. On July 10 Allied forces landed in Sicily and two weeks later the Fascist Grand Council stripped Mussolini of his powers. Now Hitler showed that he was not yet finished as a decisive leader. He reacted by ordering the seizure of Rome and the evacuation of 60,000

German soldiers from Sicily. By September 8, when it became known that the Italian government had surrendered to the Allies, the Germans had occupied Rome. This meant that for the next two years the Allies would have to fight their way, painfully and slowly, up through Italy.

In January 1944 the German siege of Leningrad was lifted, and by March much of the Ukraine had been regained by the Soviet Army. Hitler responded to these reverses by sacking commanding officers on the Eastern Front. Then, on June 6, 1944, came the shattering news that Allied forces had landed in Normandy, France.

Heavily laden ships take supplies to the Allies in Normandy, June 1944. The organization behind an amphibious landing was enormous as all the troops had to have sufficient ammunition and food before they could advance.

This move took the Germans by surprise. Field Marshal Rommel, in charge of coastal defenses, was actually on his way to meet Hitler when it happened. After a sleepless night, Hitler slept late on that day and no one dared to wake him until after midday. It was already late in the day when he issued the order: "the enemy is to be annihilated at the bridgehead by the evening of June 6." By then the Allies had established themselves on the beaches and vast amounts of ammunition and troops were being landed.

For the next few weeks there was confusion and dissent between Hitler and his army's high command. Now a group of senior officers, politicians and priests decided that there was no chance of negotiating a peace while Hitler was still alive: the *Führer* had to be assassinated. Since Hitler's rise to power there had been several conspiracies against him, and first attempts to kill him failed because the bombs did not go off as planned or because Hitler changed his schedule at the last moment. However, on July 20 Claus von Stauffenberg managed to place a bomb in a brief-case under a table at Hitler's headquarters in East Prussia. Hitler was studying a map spread out over this table and when von Stauffenberg heard the bomb explode, he assumed that Hitler was dead, flying to Berlin to alert the other conspirators. But Hitler was only slightly injured and at 1 am on July 21 he made a radio broadcast: "We will settle accounts the way we National Socialists are used to settling them." Immediately, hundreds of suspected anti-Nazis were rounded up and by the end of July 21, 160 officers had been executed.

Rommel was among the conspirators, but Hitler could not afford to have people know about this most popular general's opposition to him. Rommel was allowed to take his own life on October 14, and then given a state funeral.

Though shaken, Hitler spoke of the "miracle" that had saved him, a "sign from Heaven" that he would win the war. But he was even more suspicious of his generals, overriding them to make Himmler commander of army reserves and Goebbels commissioner for total war. Germany was fast running out of supplies. The Allies were getting closer and closer, and their bombers were hitting Germany's factories and oil refineries. The production of aircraft fuel was dropping. In August 1944 the Soviets took the Romanian oilfields. In the west, the Allies swept through northern France and Paris was liberated on August 25. Belgium was reclaimed in September, and then the Allied offensive became bogged down in muddy stretches of Holland. When an airborne operation to capture a bridge across the Rhine at Arnhem failed, the Allied advance was halted.

In Poland the Soviet Army moved closer and closer to the capital, Warsaw. Its people rose up to resist the Germans, and by August 6 they controlled most of the city. Hitler responded by sending in reinforcements, including units of the Waffen SS, to suppress the rising. The Soviet Army stopped short of the city and for two months Warsaw's population suffered terribly.

The German "victories" at Arnhem and Warsaw gave Hitler a breathing space in which to plan a final offensive. Despite headaches, toothaches, jaundice

THE BATTLE OF THE BULGE

On the morning of December 16 1944, the German Army launched a surprise offensive through the Ardennes Forest. US forces in and around Bastogne resisted heroically throughout the offensive and, after 10 days, the German advance was halted short of the Meuse. The Americans call this the Battle of the Bulge because of the large bulge the Germans created in the Allied front line. By the new year it had been flattened out and the Allies launched the final onslaught.

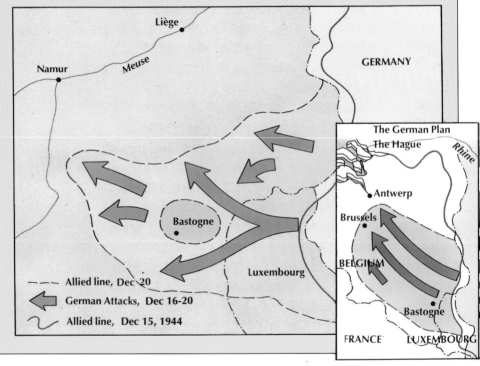

Liège

Namur

Meuse

GERMANY

Bastogne

Luxembourg

- - - Allied line, Dec 20
← German Attacks, Dec 16-20
〜 Allied line, Dec 15, 1944

The German Plan

The Hague

Rhine

Antwerp

Brussels

BELGIUM

Bastogne

FRANCE   LUXEMBOURG

and other ailments, he managed to pull himself together. He decided that a successful attack against the Allies in the west might shake them into making a new alliance against the Soviet Union. This was a gamble but, a few days before the offensive, Hitler told his commanders that they had to "make it plain to the enemy that no matter what he does he can never count on a surrender, never, never."

On December 16 the well-prepared Germans launched a surprise attack through the Ardennes. Bad weather stopped the Allies from using their air force and the German tank divisions did succeed in breaking through the Allied lines at several points. But within a few days the German offensive literally ran out of fuel and tanks were abandoned as the troops retreated on foot.

On the Eastern Front the Soviet armies launched an offensive on January 12, 1945. Within a few days they had taken Warsaw and days later they took most of East Prussia. Hitler refused to evacuate any troops from there and so some 200,000 German troops were captured. The Soviet forces were also making great advances farther south, and by the end of January they were only 99 mi from Berlin.

Hitler returned to Berlin, making his last base in a concrete bunker underneath the Chancellery. He was finding it more and more difficult to control his rages, quarreling with his chief of staff, Heinz Guderian, and dismissing him. He made his last radio broadcast to the German people on January 30, 1945. Still he deluded himself that all was not lost: "We shall overcome this emergency also." For the next three months Hitler seldom appeared above ground and one observer noted how: "he dragged himself about painfully and clumsily. . . he had lost his sense of balance. . . saliva frequently dripped from the corners of his mouth." Now he fell out with such close associates as Göring and Ribbentrop, and he drew his only comfort from one of Blondi's puppies and quantities of chocolate and cream cakes. But on April 12, when he heard of the sudden death of the President, Franklin Roosevelt, he began to have fantasies about victory again: "Here we have the miracle I always predicted. . . . The war isn't lost." But this hopefulness was short-lived. On the Western Front the Allies had taken the Ruhr, Germany's industrial heartland. On April 16 the Russians launched their attack on Berlin.

As Germany was destroyed by Allied bombs, German troops in retreat added to the destruction, on Hitler's orders. There would be nothing left of Germany but scorched earth: the Third Reich would die with its *Führer*. On April 20 he celebrated his 56th birthday with leading Nazis: Göring, Goebbels, Himmler, Bormann, Speer and others. Eva Braun was also present and Hitler seemed in good spirits. But he was not sure what to do next. Should he abandon Berlin and withdraw to the Bavarian Alps, or should he die fighting to defend the city? On that same day most of the Nazi leaders left Berlin.

Within hours Soviet shells were falling on Berlin and Hitler found the energy to order a last attempt to repel the attack. But by the next day he realized that this was impossible and fell into one of his rages, denouncing the traitors in the army and talking of his own suicide. During the next few days he was subject to many violent changes of mood. On April 23 Göring infuriated him by asking if he should assume leadership of the government and on April 28 he heard that Himmler was trying to negotiate peace. He decided to end it all. In a hasty ceremony he married Eva Braun. On April 30, following the usual morning conference and lunch, he retired to his rooms with his new wife.

Shortly before 4 pm a single shot was heard and when SS bodyguards entered the room they found Hitler shot in the head and Eva Braun poisoned. According to Hitler's strict instructions, the guards then burned the bodies. On that very day the Soviet Army took Berlin.

On May 4 and 7 Admiral Hans von Friedeburg and General Jodl signed Germany's unconditional surrender and World War II in Europe was over. By this time most of the Nazi leaders were either dead or under arrest. More than ten million German soldiers were in captivity and the civilian population was starving and desperate. Germany was occupied by the Soviet, American, British and French armies. The Allies discovered the concentration camps full of dying or starving people, as well as corpses, and the full horror of Hitler's Third Reich became known to the world.

Hitler with his dog Blondi and Eva Braun. Hitler kept her in the background. He married her shortly before their joint suicide.

CHRONOLOGY

1889 Adolf Hitler born at Braunau in Austria.

1903 Hitler's father dies.

1905 Hitler leaves school.

1907 Hitler goes to live in Vienna; his mother dies.

1914 World War I starts: Germany and Austria-Hungary are at war with Russia, France and Great Britain; Hitler becomes a regimental runner in the German Army.

1918 World War I ends.

1919 An armed uprising in Berlin and chaos throughout Germany; the Treaty of Versailles is signed; Germany loses 13 percent of its territory; Hitler leaves the army and joins the German Workers' Party.

1921 Hitler becomes the leader of the Nazi Party.

1922 Mussolini marches on Rome and seizes power in Italy.

1923 Hitler's Beer Hall Putsch in Munich fails.

1924 Hitler is sent to jail, where he writes *Mein Kampf*; released after nine months.

1925 Hindenburg elected president of Germany; Hitler begins to rebuild the Nazi Party.

1928 Nazi Party wins 12 seats in elections to the *Reichstag*.

1930 Nazi Party wins 107 seats in elections to the *Reichstag*.

1932 Hindenburg defeats Hitler in the German presidential elections; Nazi Party wins 230 seats in *Reichstag* elections.

1933 Hitler becomes the German chancellor; fire at the *Reichstag*; the Enabling Act is passed and Hitler becomes a dictator.

1934 Night of the Long Knives sees the destruction of the SA and many of Hitler's personal enemies; Hindenburg dies and Hitler becomes president.

1935 Nuremberg laws introduced – the persecution of the Jews begins.

1936 Germany sends troops into the Rhineland.

1937 Italy joins the

German-Japanese pact against communism.

1938 *Anschluss* – Germany annexes Austria; the Munich Agreement is signed and Hitler sends in troops to occupy Czechoslovakia's Sudetenland.

1939 Germany annexes the rest of Czechoslovakia; September, Germany invades Poland – the beginning of World War II.

1940 April, Germany invades Denmark and Norway; May – June, Germany defeats France, Belgium and the Netherlands; September, Battle of Britain at its height; December, British troops begin to drive Italians out of Egypt.

1941 April, Germany defeats Yugoslavia and Greece; June, Germany invades the Soviet Union; December, Germany fails to take Moscow and Hitler declares war on the United States after the Japanese attack on Pearl Harbor.

1942 The mass extermination of the Jewish people begins; May, the Germans launch a new offensive in the southern territory of the Soviet Union; September, the Germans reach Stalingrad;

November, Germans defeated at El Alamein in Egypt and Allied landings in North Africa.

1943 February, the Germans surrender at Stalingrad; May, final surrender of German and Italian troops in Tunisia; July, the German Army is defeated at the Battle of Kursk and the Soviet Union launches a major counterattack; September, Allied landings in Italy; November, the Soviets retake Kiev.

1944 January, siege of Leningrad is lifted; March, Soviet troops enter Romania; June, the Allied forces land in Normandy (D-Day) and the Soviets launch their offensive in Belorussia; July, the Bomb Plot against Hitler fails; August, Paris is liberated; September, the Allies' progress across western Europe slows down; December, the Germans counterattack in the Ardennes.

1945 March, Anglo-American troops cross the Rhine; April, Mussolini is killed by partisans and Hitler commits suicide in his bunker in Berlin; May, Germany formally surrenders – the end of the war in Europe; August, Japan surrenders – the end of World War II.

GLOSSARY

Allies the countries that fought against Germany, Italy and Japan during World War II – Great Britain, France, the United States, the Soviet Union and China.

Anschluss the annexation of Austria by Germany, 1938.

anti-Semitic being hostile to Jewish people.

Axis the agreement signed in September 1940 between Germany, Italy and Japan. Romania, Bulgaria, Slovakia and Hungary joined later.

Blitzkrieg lightning war – mobile armored warfare.

Bolshevik the name of the Communist Party that seized power in Russia in 1917.

Chancellor the German equivalent of prime minister.

communism the belief that all property – including land and industry – should be owned by the community rather than by individuals.

democracy government by the people, through elected representatives.

dictator someone who takes all power into his own hands and does not allow democracy.

fascism has come to mean anyone with extreme right-wing views. It was used to describe the regimes of Mussolini and Hitler. Fascism was not a set of beliefs but more attitudes, for example, obedience to the leader.

Final Solution the phrase used by the Nazis to describe the extermination of the Jewish people.

Freikorps (Free Corps) right-wing volunteer units used by the German government in 1918 to keep order.

Gleichschaltung coordination or streamlining. The process of putting everything under Nazi control.

Marxism the 19th-century belief that the workers were oppressed by the ruling classes and would rise up in a revolution. Karl Marx expounded his ideas in a book called *Das Kapital*.

nationalism the belief that one's country should be allowed to govern itself. Hitler took this to an extreme form.

propaganda misleading information arranged and distorted by a group trying to win people over to its point of view.

Putsch a coup – when someone tries to seize power by using violence and breaking the law.

Prussia the leading state or region within Germany.

Reichstag the German parliament.

socialism the belief that income and wealth needs to be distributed fairly.

Third Reich Hitler's rule of Germany. The First Reich was the Holy Roman Empire in the Middle Ages. The Second Reich lasted from 1871-1918, when Germany was united under the rule of the kings of Prussia.

Weimar Republic Germany's brief attempt at democracy from the end of World War I to Hitler's Third Reich.

FURTHER READING

Bullock, A *Hitler. A Study in Tyranny*, Harper & Rew, 1971

Calvocoressi, Peter and Wint, Guy *Total War: Causes and Courses of the Second War*, Partheon, 1980

Carsten, F. L. *The Rise of Fascism*, University of California Press, 1980

Gordon, Sarah *Hitler, Germans and the Jewish Question* Princeton University Press, 1984

Kershaw, Ian *"Hitler Myth" Image and Reality in the Third Reich* Oxford University Press, 1989

Krantz, Morris and Auster Louise *Hitler's Death March* Zebra, 1980

Nicholls, A.J. *Weimer and the Rise of Hitler, 2nd ed* St, Martin, 1980

Schirer, W.L. *The Rise and Fall of Adolph Hitler* Random House, 1963

Speer, A. *Inside the Third Reich* Macmillan, 1981

Spielvogel, Jackson J. *Hitler and Nazi Germany: A History* Prentice-Hall, 1988

Stern, J.P. *Hitler: The Fuhrer and the People*, University of California Press, 1975

INDEX

Photographic Credits:
Cover and pages 12 and 30: Zefa; page 4: Hulton Picture Company; pages 6, 7, 11, 16, 19, 20, 25, 42, 43, 48 bottom, 51 and 57: Popperfoto; pages 29 top and bottom, 35, 38 and 40: Signal; page 48 top: USAF.